listening to cement

photographs by robert stivers

essay by john stauffer

ARENA EDITIONS

The life which is unexamined is not worth living.
—PLATO

Man is a creature who makes pictures of himself,
and then comes to resemble the picture.
—IRIS MURDOCH

SOMETHING SEEMS OUT OF PLACE when you first meet Robert Stivers. He is one of the foremost contemporary photographers, whose work has appeared in galleries and museums from New York and London to Cologne. He has been written about and discussed in the *New Yorker*, the *Village Voice*, and *Art News*. And this is his second book of photographs in three years. But he carries his success in a quiet, unassuming way. In an age of irony and cynicism, of bravado and swagger, of slick surface effects with little depth, he prefers the qualities of sincerity and wonder, subtlety and nuance, hard work and endurance. He is an intellectual who is not haughty, and an artist who refuses to use theoretical jargon to promote his work. He is an artist, in other words, who embraces the love of craft, does not try to hide the sweat that makes his vision a reality, and revels in the open-ended creative process that is part and parcel of his work.

The images that follow are a testimony to this ethic. Stivers views art as synonymous with artisanship. He prides himself on being self-taught, spends most of his time in the darkroom, and believes that ninety percent of the creative process occurs there. This is in contrast to many of his peers—often formally trained—who do not even print their own work. The results are startling: the rich textures and tones in his work are virtually unparalleled in the history of the medium. And taken together, these images seek to elevate art—and the self—

to the realm of the spiritual; they are mysterious, darkly romantic, sensual, and sublime. His is a unique and original vision at a time when many critics and artists have lost faith in the originality of the artist and the uniqueness of the art object.

In these pages, Stivers extends and deepens the search for identity that occupied him in his first book, *Robert Stivers: Photographs* (Arena Editions, 1997). The themes of mystery and movement reflect his continual search for self-understanding. He bares his soul in these images; indeed he considers all of his work a form of self-portraiture, from the early, sharply focused self-representations of the 1980s to these richly textured and out-of-focus images of statues and architecture, people and places. By juxtaposing the human figure with architectural images, he points to the reciprocity between consciousness and a sense of place that is central to an understanding of the self. In Stivers's vision, nothing is ever static; there is constant movement and continual flux, not only of the self but also of time and place. Ultimately, his vision speaks to the possibilities and limits of the American dream of self-transformation, a theme that has preoccupied photographers from Mathew Brady to Cindy Sherman. But to understand and fully appreciate Stivers's vision, we need to know something about the self to which his work indirectly refers.

In many respects, Stivers has lived three lives, and all of them are richly conveyed in his work. The first was as a ballet dancer, a remarkable achievement in itself given his background, upbringing, and late start. He grew up in California, the only son in an upper-middle-class family of academics and corporate executives. His father, an early survivor of spinal meningitis, was proclaimed dead at age fourteen but went on to receive a Ph.D. in civil engineering from Stanford and to have an illustrious career as an aerospace engineer. His mother graduated Phi Beta Kappa and summa cum laude from Stanford. One sister entered the ranks of the corporate elite, and the other sister became a clinical and social psychologist. From his family's perspective, Robert was the wayward son. After graduating from UC-Irvine in 1976, he dropped out of a master's program in the science of administration because he was spending all his time dancing. He had been dancing for only a few years, and his parents viewed it as frivolous, if not a bit unseemly. In 1979 he and his girlfriend moved to New York City, and within two years he had performed with the Joffrey Ballet. His dancing career ended abruptly after he suffered a horrible back injury (which still bothers him).

His second life was as a stockbroker/life insurance agent, which was not a healthy environment for him. It is a profession that requires no formal degree and no rigorous training. There are few barriers to entry, and unlike the arts it involves little adherence to craft or the process of production. Perhaps he became a broker to appease his parents and conform to their model of respectability. No matter what the motives, he tried to fill the void left by his death as a dancer with wine, and by the late 1980s, drinking—an occupational hazard among brokers—was consuming his life. In 1988, during the depths of his despair, he woke up one morning and felt that "something had shifted." The desire and need for drink had suddenly vanished (and hasn't returned). He had already become interested in photography and had established a number of friends who were photographers. In the wake of his epiphany, when "something shifted" within him, he quit his job and devoted his life to photography and the quest to re-create himself through his art.

The three lives of Robert Stivers are infused and juxtaposed in his work. The movement of dance is evoked by his out-of-focus images, his attention to line and form in the figures—some of them actual dancers—and his expressive use of the human body. The troubled, anxious, and haunting world of the broker, vision impaired by drink, is there as well. And his technical virtuosity as a photographer fills every image. But what makes these images so haunting and mysterious is that Stivers attempts to render visually the process of self-transformation. He shows through his aesthetics the death and rebirth of the self and the void of disorientation that accompanies this evolution. Portraits and places intersect, and figures dance around and through columns and curves of stone. In Stivers's vision, as in his life, everything is in a state of continuous flux and has the capability of being transformed: Negatives of statues become living portraits; people are transformed into art; and inanimate objects acquire a personality and life of their own.

Stivers's three lives represent a harrowing set of transformative experiences; they are unaccountable and mysterious, but ultimately uplifting. So too are his images. The "something" that shifted in him—led him out of the abyss to photography and an aesthetic reality, and eventually these images—can perhaps best be described as spiritual. He experienced a "letting go," as he phrased it, of a material world defined by fixed markers and rigid boundaries, and he sought to connect with a transcendent spirit world and cosmos. In these images, the boundaries between positive and negative space are necessarily blurred. Figures and statues, buildings and columns acquire a new look, a new feel; they bend, extend, and intersect with the space and objects around them. In almost every image there is a zone of indeterminacy between the foreground and background, underscoring Stivers's quest to transcend a material world of fixity and stasis.

The images here offer the fullest expression of self-transformation and the quest for transcendence in Stivers's oeuvre—and possibly among contemporary photographers as a whole. In his earliest series of images in the late 1980s, Stivers reenacted the self-destructive behavior to which he had succumbed as a broker. One self-portrait shows him lying on a bed of nails; in another image he points a gun to his chest, as if to destroy the self and the life force (as well as the erection that appears in the image). These early images symbolized an outdated self that needed to be destroyed (or at least punished) before rebirth could occur. The regeneration that followed these elegies and penances took shape as a mysterious, darkly romantic, and sublime identity, which he has continued to develop and refine.

Since his first book, Stivers has gained a greater critical distance from which to analyze his three lives, and thus incorporate them into his compositions. The interaction between subjectivity and environment in this book reflects a newfound willingness to let chance and fate have their say. As a result, he has a deeper understanding of who he is and where he has been. As Stivers himself acknowledges, his early work tended toward exhibition-ism and confrontation. Although it would be a gross exaggeration to say that he is now at peace with himself, he admits that "knowing about who I am" requires grappling with the "history of who I was." He is no longer afraid to explore his past selves, and he acknowledges the close links between past and present. "History is always the interpretation of the present," the philosopher George Herbert Mead noted, and the present is always the vantage point from which we interpret and make sense of the past. This interplay between past and present applies to the self as much as to art, culture, and society. Significantly, many of the images in this book derive from some of Stivers's earliest negatives. In other words, the building blocks and raw materials have remained the same, but the aesthetic vision and realization of it are totally new. Quite literally, then, he draws on experience and critical distance to fuse past and present.

Stivers exposes his anxieties and desire for transcendence more poignantly than just about any other liv-ing artist. These images are profoundly empathic. He seeks to collapse (or at least blur) the barriers between subject and object, form and content, self and other, the viewer and the work. Through this quest for empathy comes the possibility for redemption. Stivers's work suggests that after searching for our identity in contemporary America, we discover a deep void. But it is a void that can be filled by the wonderment and mystery of an unseen spiritual world. As we face a new millennium and look back on a ravaged century, these images offer an antidote to the loss of faith in transcendence and to the over-rehearsed axioms that God is dead and that there is no autonomous self. Stivers's life exposes a self that refuses to lie still; it is polymorphous and capable of being liberated from material circumstances. Through his art he opens up for us an identity—both individual and collective—that can accept wonder as well as worry, faith as well as doubt. He creates an alternative reality, an aesthetic self that is large and contains multitudes, to paraphrase Walt Whitman, and he invites us to participate in his darkly romantic vision. Both the life and the art are extraordinary accomplishments.

JOHN STAUFFER

Harvard University

April 2000

listening to cement

plates

PLATE 1

PLATE 2

PLATE 3

PLATE 4

PLATE 5

PLATE 6

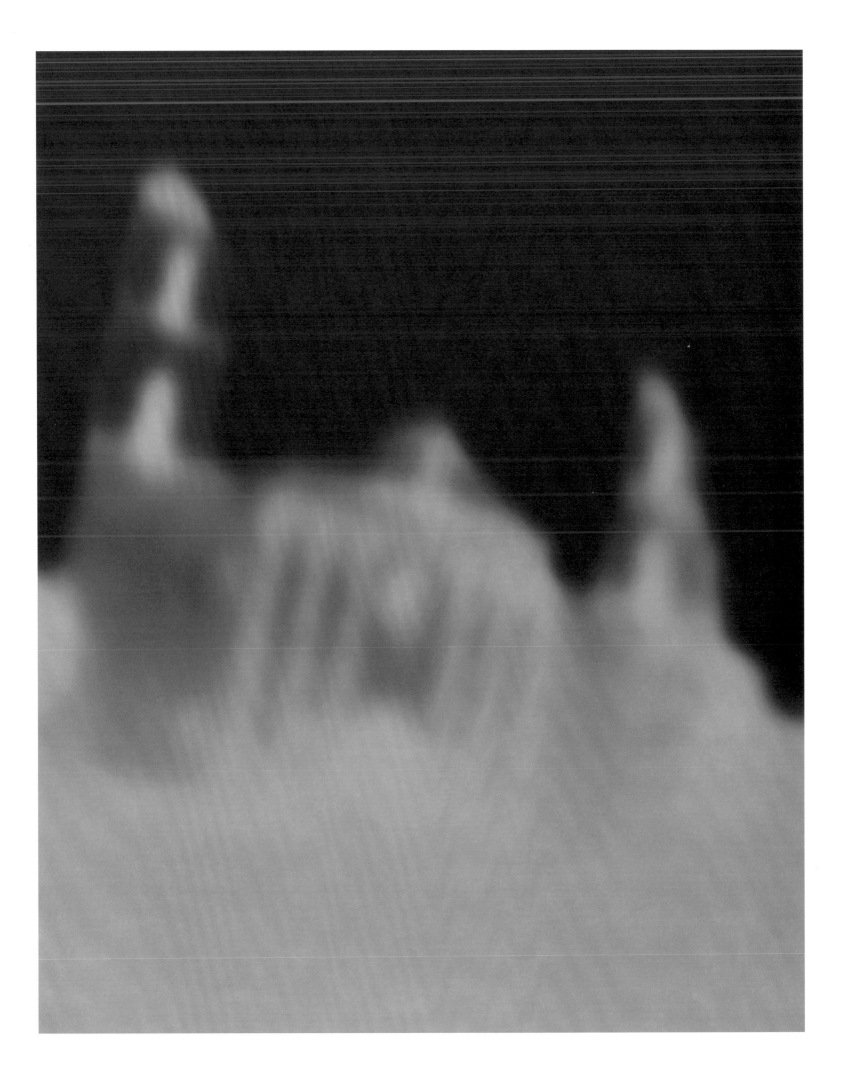

PLATE 7

PLATE 8

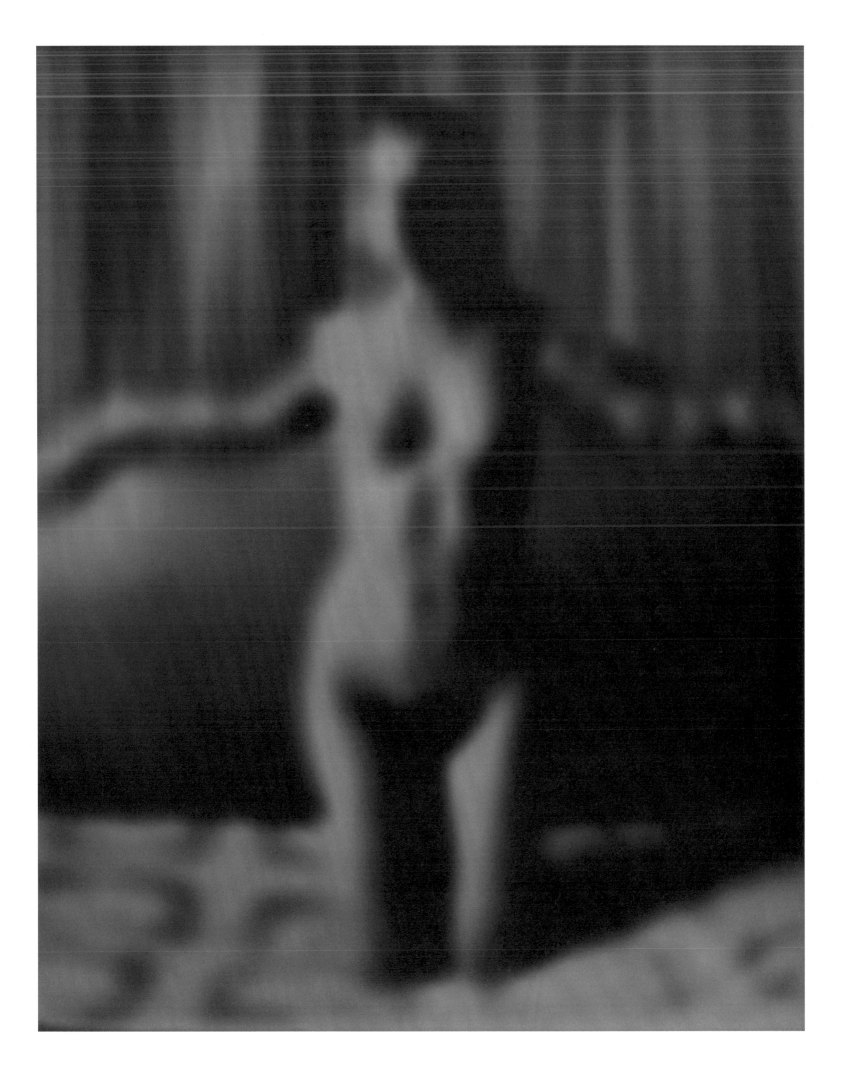

PLATE 9

PLATE 10

PLATE 11

PLATE 12

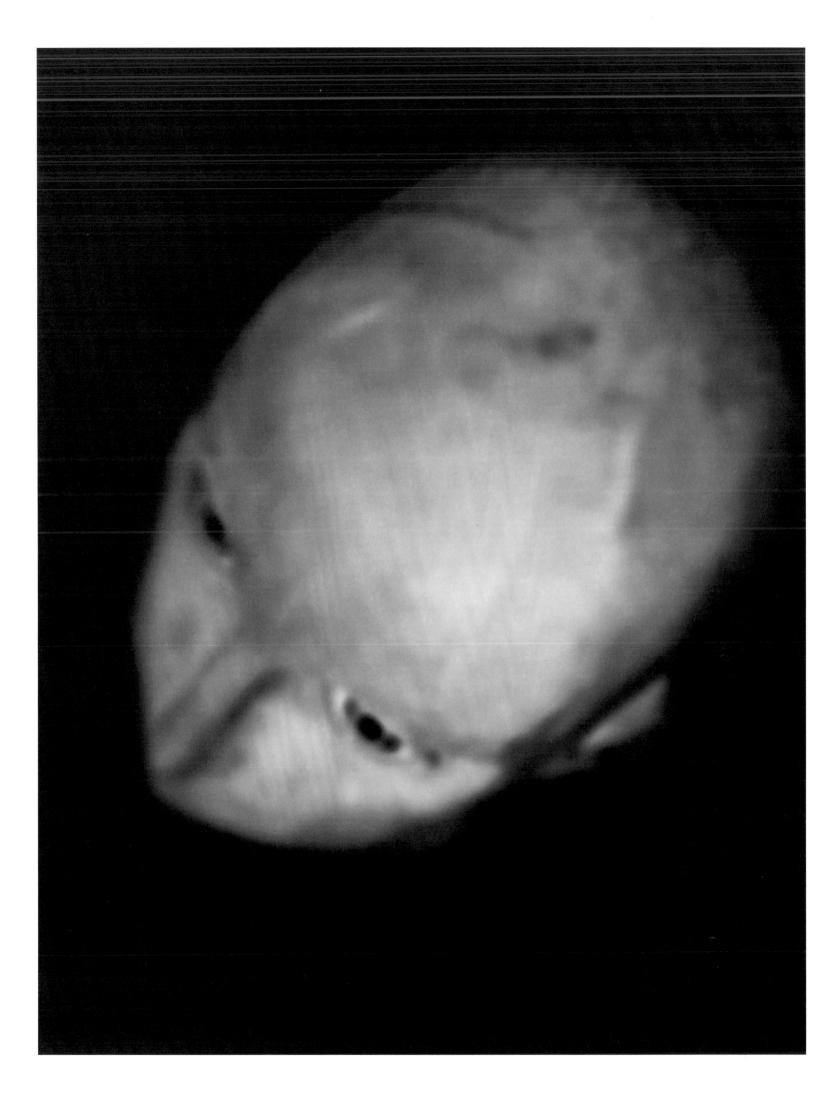

PLATE 13

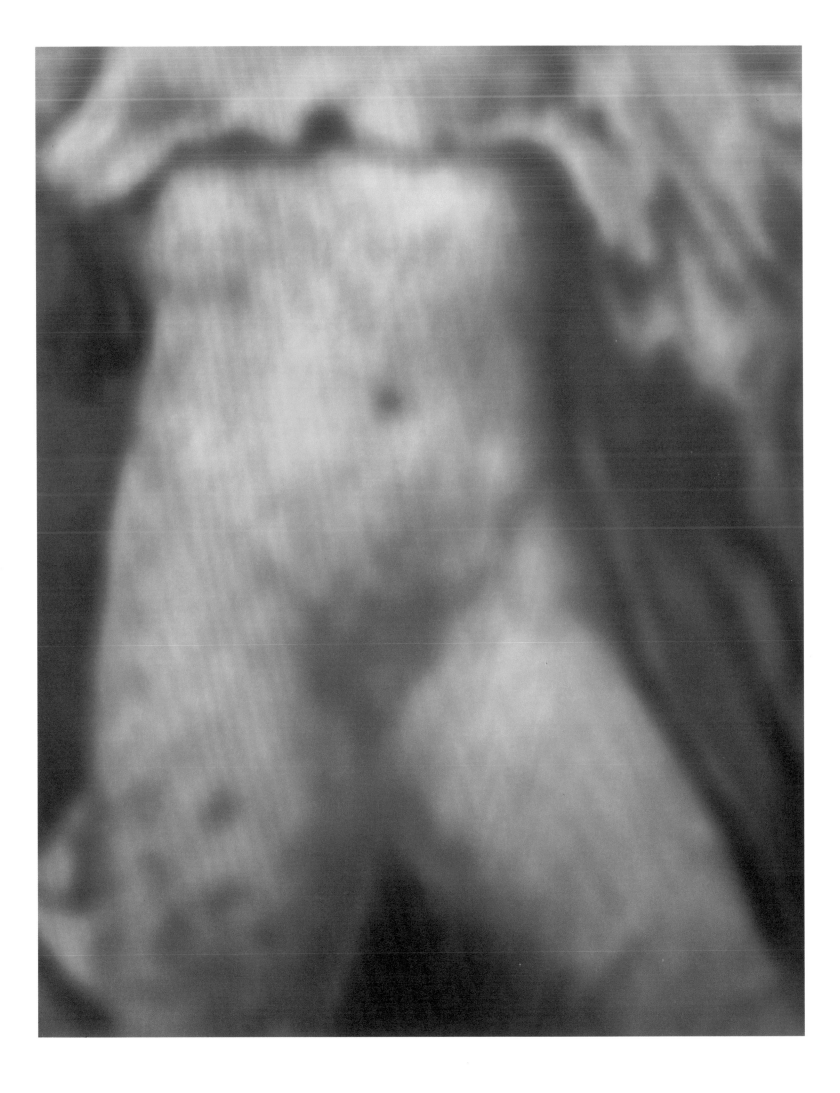

PLATE 14

PLATE 15

PLATE 16

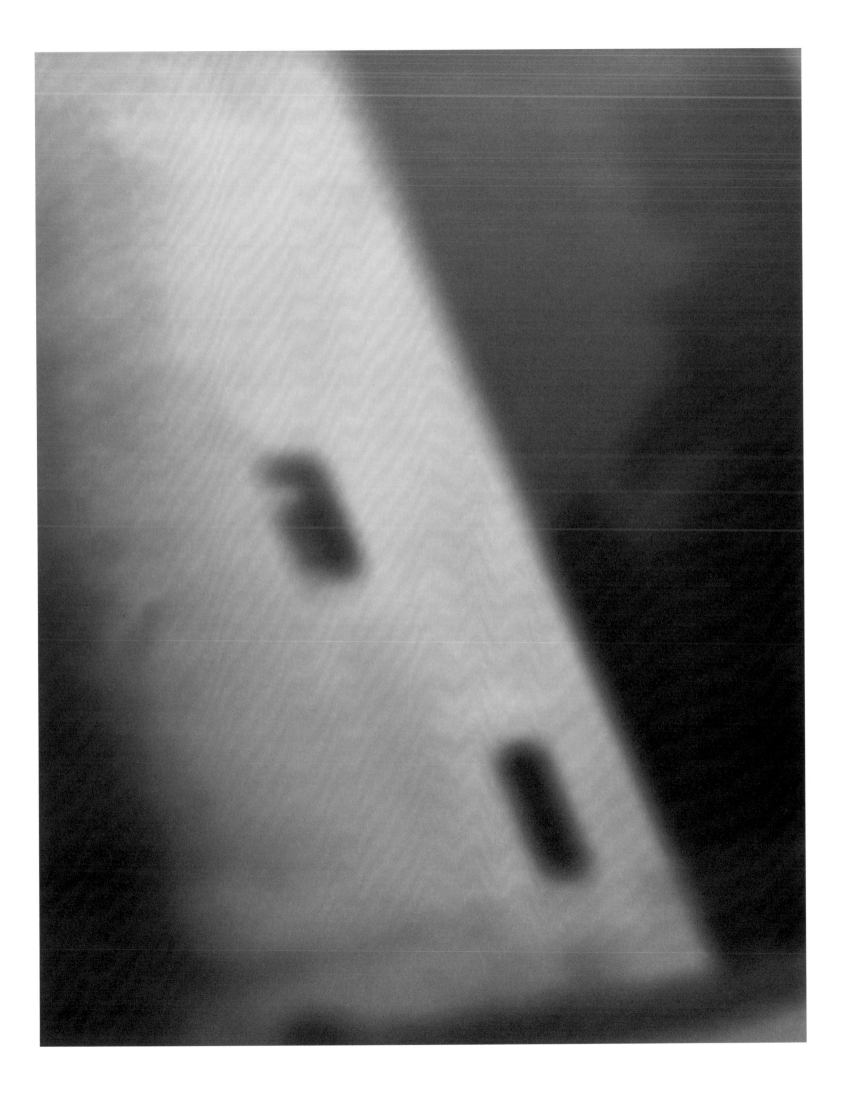

PLATE 17

PLATE 18

PLATE 19

PLATE 20

PLATE 21

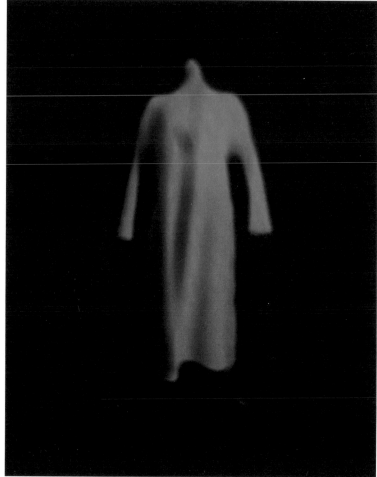

PLATE 22

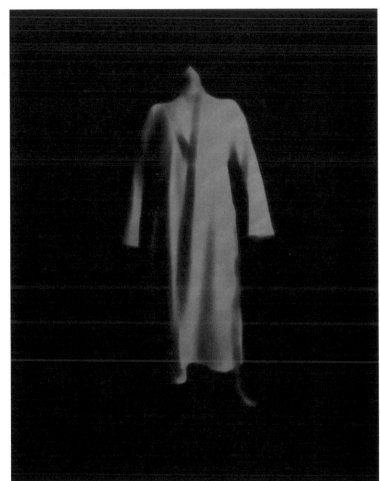

PLATE 23

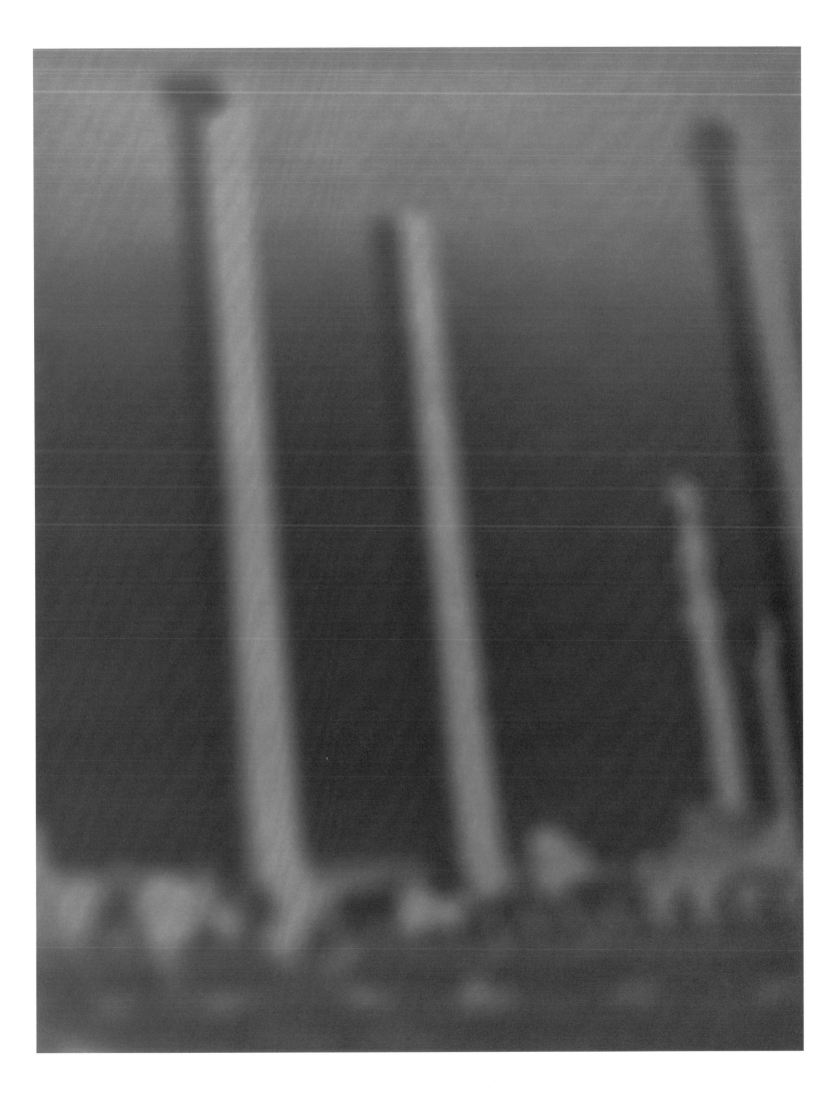

PLATE 24

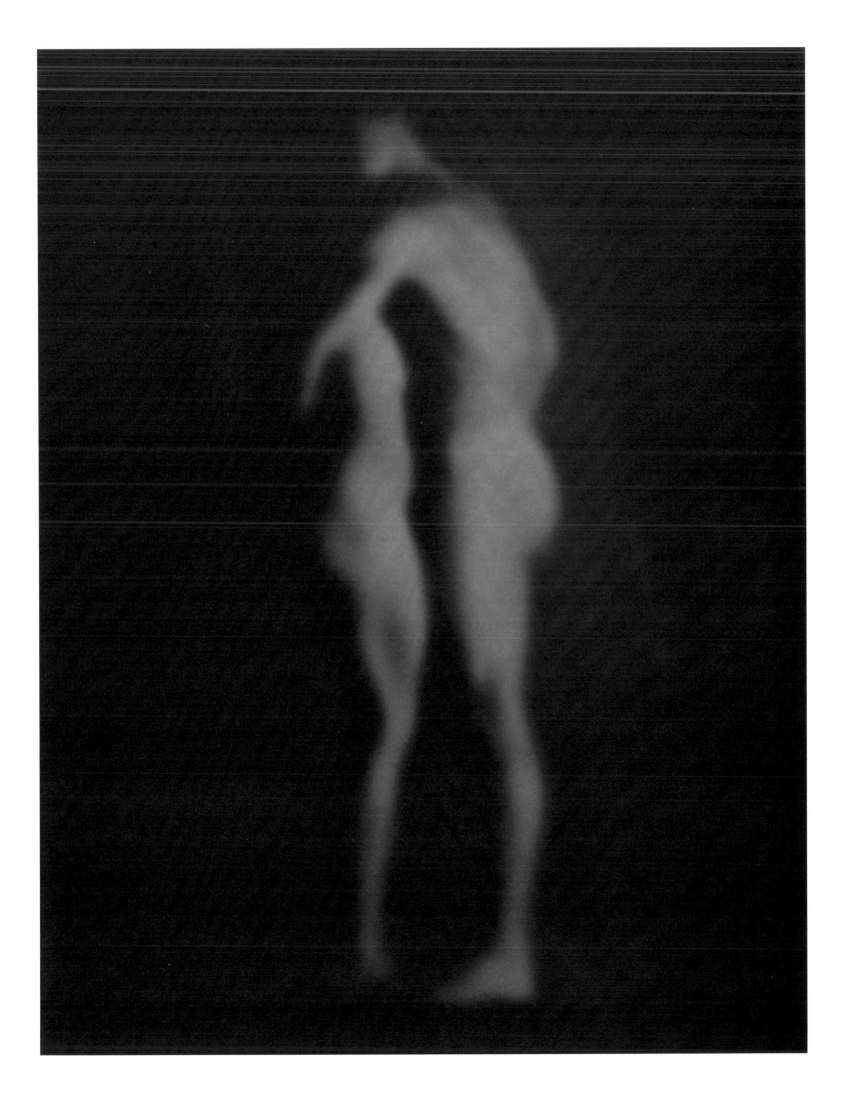

PLATE 25

PLATE 26

PLATE 27

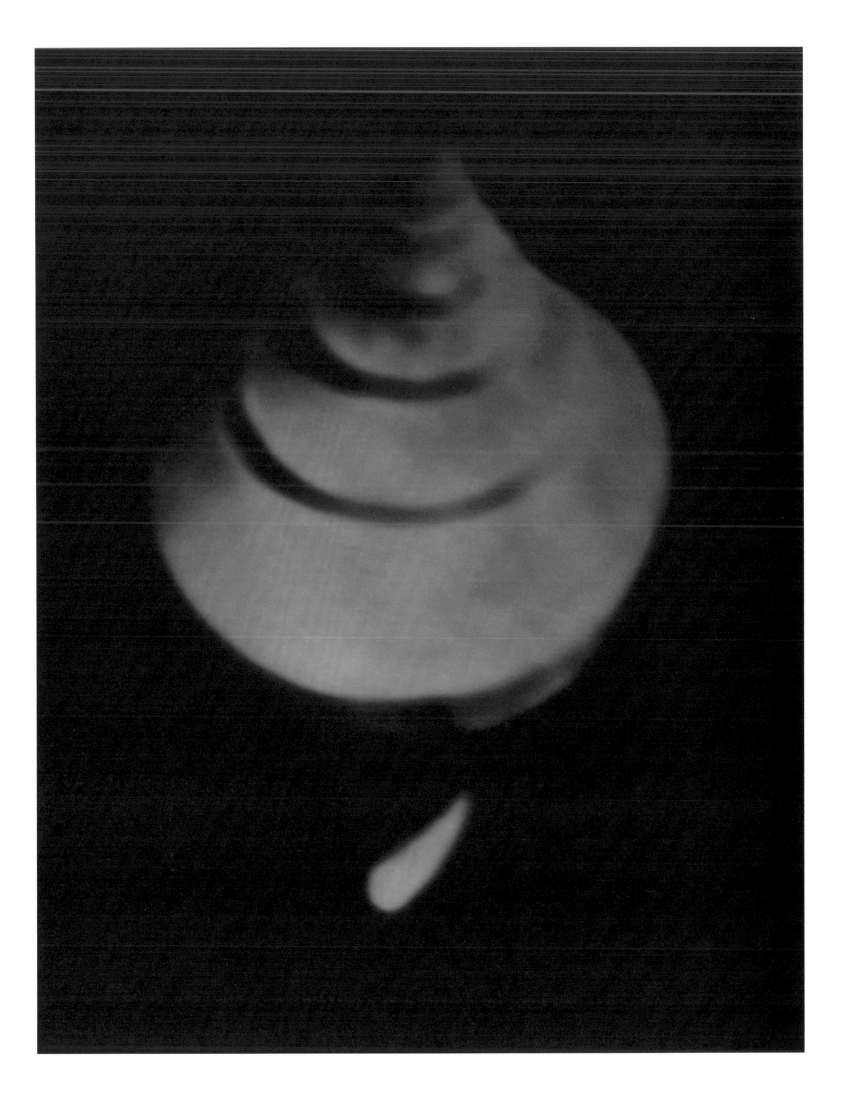

PLATE 28

PLATE 29

PLATE 30

PLATE 31

PLATE 32

PLATE 33

PLATE 34

PLATE 35

PLATE 36

PLATE 37

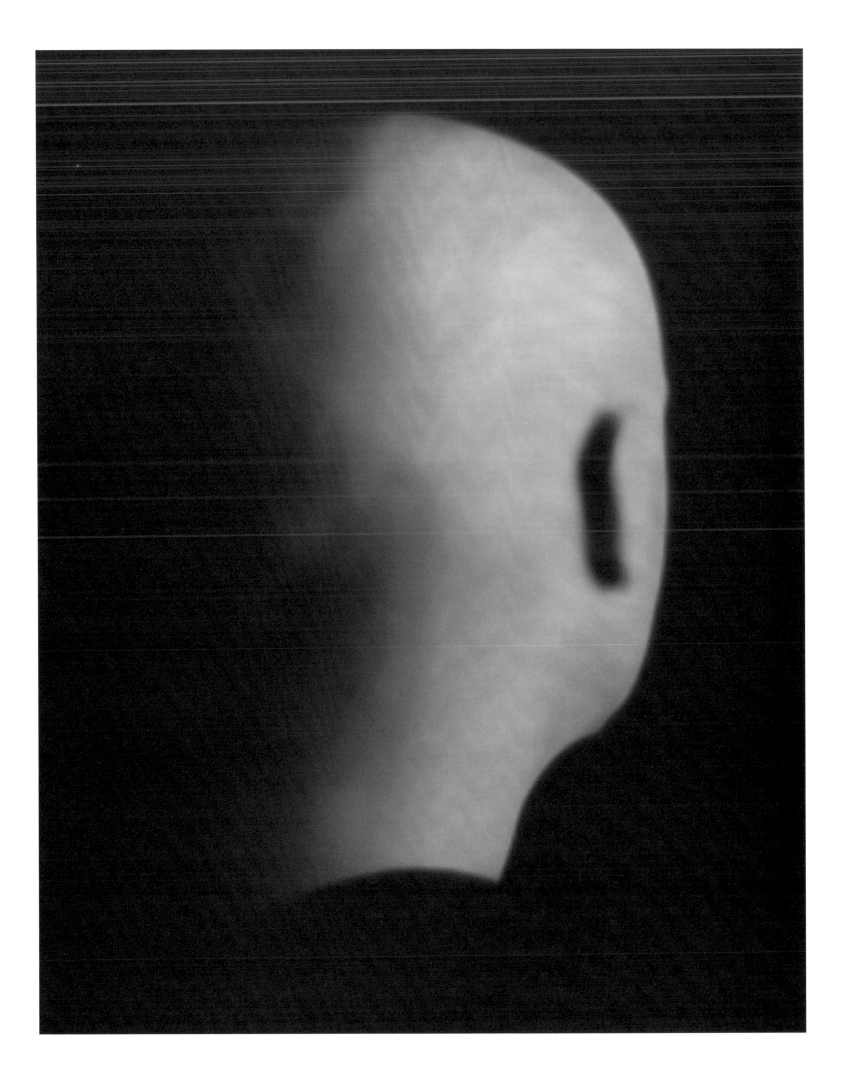

PLATE 38

PLATE 39

PLATE 40

PLATE 41

PLATE 42

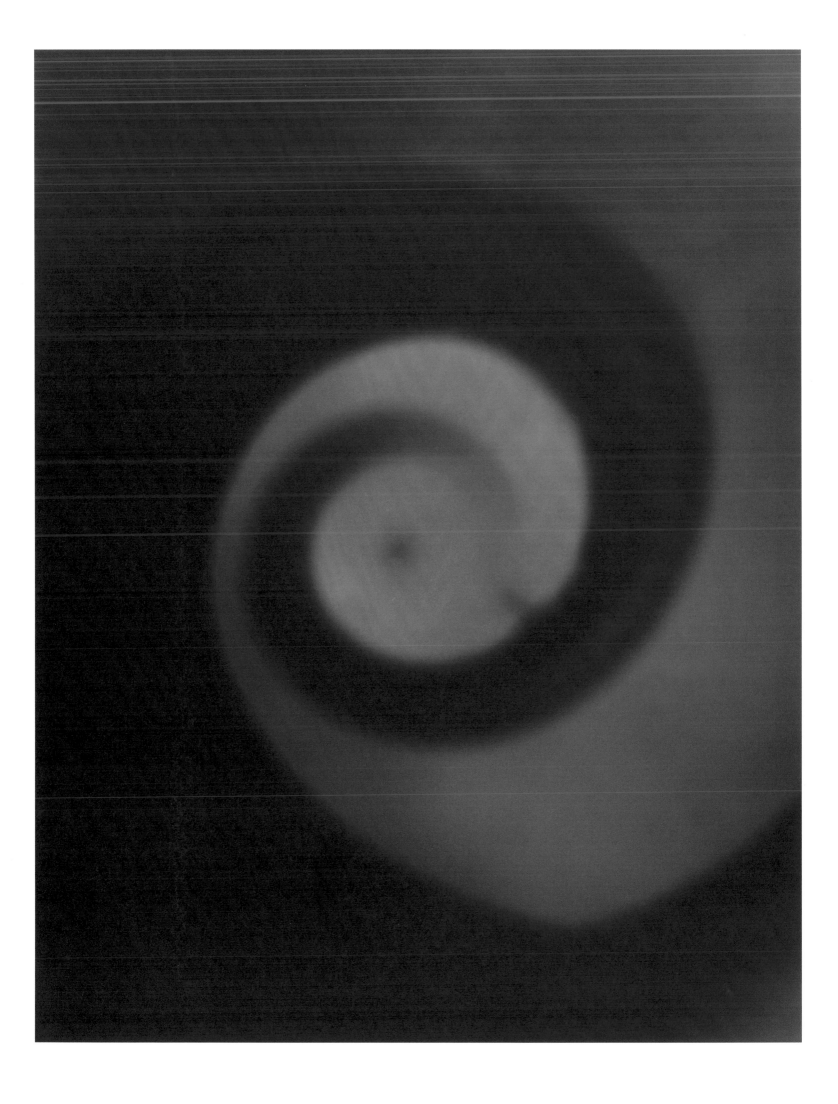

PLATE 43

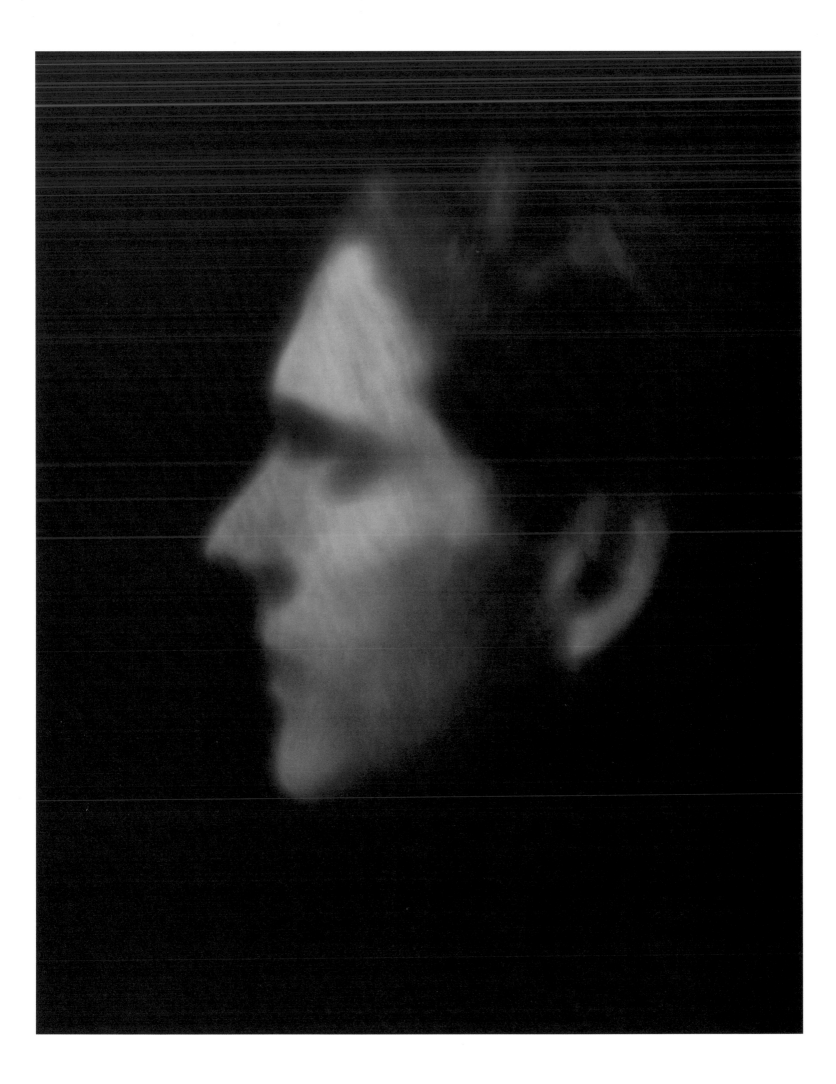

PLATE 44

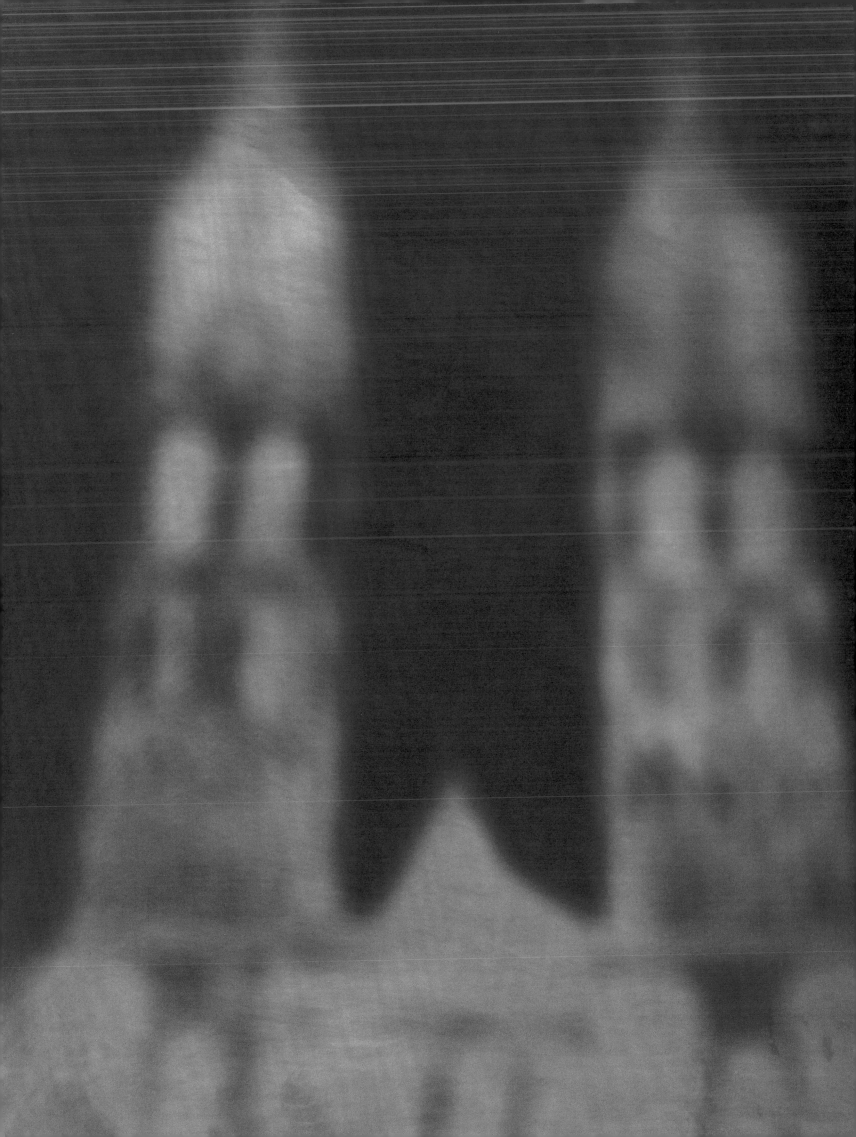

PLATE 45

PLATE 46

First edition published by Arena Editions
P.O. Box 32101
Santa Fe, New Mexico 87594-2101
USA

Phone 505-986-9132
Fax 505-986-9138

www.arenaeditions.com

Publishing Concept: James Crump
Book Design: David Skolkin

Printed by EBS – Verona, Italy

First Edition, 2000

Library of Congress Control Number: 00-132761
ISBN 1-892041-33-2

WORDS OF ACKNOWLEDGEMENT
Deep gratitude and thanks to those who have given their time, supported me unconditionally, and generously provided me with inspiration.